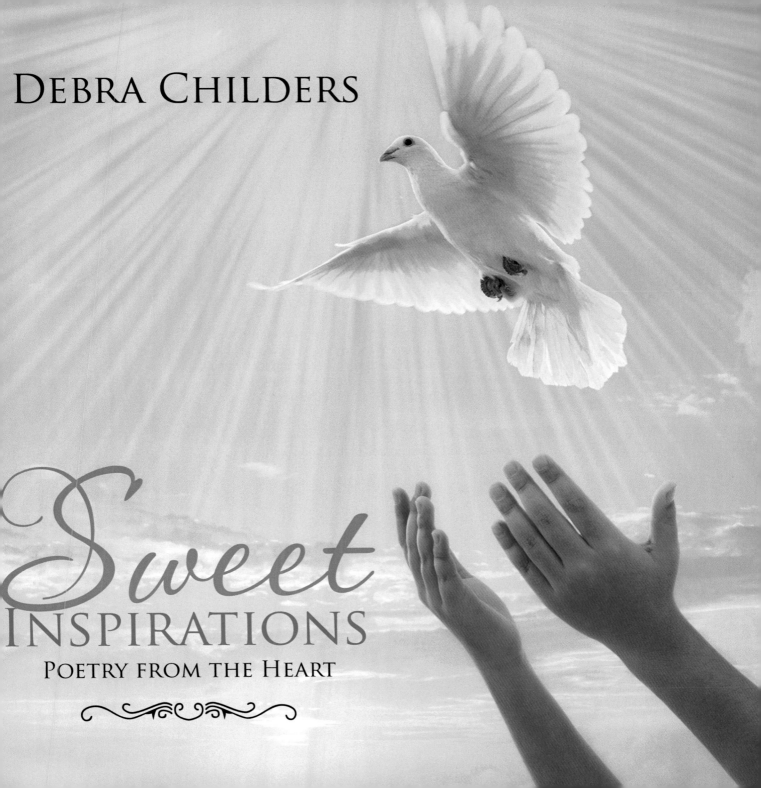

DEBRA CHILDERS

Sweet
INSPIRATIONS
POETRY FROM THE HEART

To order additional copies of this book, contact:
Xlibris LLC
1-888-795-4274
www.Xlibris.com
Orders@Xlibris.com

TABLE OF CONTENTS

Joy

Joy is waking up with Peace of mind
Joy is having a pure and clean heart
Joy is having Freedom, and being kind
Joy is knowing Salvation in Jesus
Joy is knowing that from the start
Jesus' love for us will not depart

The Comforter

God has made a way possible
For man to endure hardship and pain
It is through his Holy Spirit
That rest is found among the wearied
We can overcome when needed most
Through the power of the Holy Ghost

It Is Well

Be not discouraged, be not dismayed
Be not weary, nor be afraid
Be not sad, but be glad
Be of good cheer, wear a smile
For it will tell that all is well

Chosen

Even before you are born, you're thought of
For you are chosen, by our Father above
Special gems to him, are we
For this reason, he came to set us free
To us he offers eternal life
He gives us freewill, do or die.
For this reason, the choice is ours
Yes, that's right, it's up to us
To have life eternal, or to remain unjust

Reborn

You were born of a woman
For this was natural
You were born as a babe of fine stature
You were born to a union, out of compassion
And now fully grown and quite mature
You now desire to live life in a better fashion
Now you have to repent and be baptized in Jesus Name
And buried in water for the remission of sin
And born of the spirit and of water
You are now a new creature, heavenly adored
Glory Hallelujah! You've been reborn.

Blessed Quietness

Sometimes sitting alone
Enjoying the stillness
Watching the sunset
Noticing the day has gone
Meditating on things above
Thoughts racing through your mind
Joy dwells within, because of Jesus Love
Never before experiencing Joy of this kind
The inner peace, the serenity, a tranquil rest
Ahh Blessed Quietness.

A Better Way

This world is void, it shall pass away
It can offer you, nothing but despair
Seek ye the Lord, don't hesitate
The time is drawing near
Tomorrow may be too late
Be free of sin, be born again
Don't ponder over what people may say
Just boldly tell them there's a better way.

Road of Salvation

Come with me down the Road of Salvation
Many have traveled along this road
Along the way we shall have tribulations
Many have come to know, this is where peace abide
Bearing in mind that if we follow this trail
We will lift our eyes up in Heaven, and not in Hell.

Follow Jesus

Did you know that Jesus loves you?
Well he does, so much he died for us
Come unto Jesus, be made free
Consider your soul, consider your behavior
Follow Jesus, be sin free
For Jesus desires to be your Savior

Hope in Jesus

God knew that Man would fail
For Man is of flesh and bone
Jesus is whom you should seek
For He will never leave you alone
You see man is of flesh, which is weak
But in Christ Jesus we have hope
Be of good cheer endure strife
Because at the end there's everlasting Life

The Promise

Jesus came to save the soul of man
He's standing with an out stretched hand
Jesus our Savior is coming again
Depart from your evil ways
For He has given you this promise
That if you repent of your sins
And keep his commandments
And diligently seek his face
That in the end at judgment time
You shall be saved by grace.

Did you know?

Did you know
That Jesus died for you and me
That we might have eternal life you see
That He's alive and well today
His goodness and mercy will never go away
Jesus is our very best friend
He pours out blessings over and over again
Open up your heart, let him in
For righteousness is the way to go
My friend, I ask you, did you know?

A Friend in Jesus

When man turns his back on you
And you are burdened with despair
When Man lie, cheat and steal
Our friend Jesus is always near
When you are sick and in need
Man will forsake you, He will flee
The answer is just a prayer away
For Jesus is a friend indeed.

Peace be still!

Are the storms in your life raging
Are you weighted down with despair from hurt
Is there sadness instead of gladness
And are you torn inside from the madness
Look to the hills from where your help cometh
Our help is in Jesus, He hears our cry
Put your trust in him, do his will
He will send you a comforter
And you will hear a voice quietly saying
Peace be still, peace be still

The Child Jesus

God our father and creator
Thought of a plan to save us
He saw that man was weak and unfit
He knew he had to redeem us and quick
He sent his only begotten son
Born a babe unto the Virgin Mary
God knew he would get the job done
Born in Bethlehem and in a manger
To us he grew to be no stranger
Now man can be made free from sin
Through Jesus Christ our Savior and Friend

Abundance Now

Faith is what it takes to prosper
It cannot be done by money alone
Believe on me my Lord said
Trust and not doubt I am the bread
I have given you the power to get wealth
Mercy and grace is what he felt
When he said you shall have life
And have it more abundantly
Seek the Lord while He is near
Be not weary do not fear
Enjoy life you can be satisfied
Rejoice abundance now is here

Be made whole

Reach out and touch the Lord
He's the only answer today
Reach out and touch the Lord
Trust him, he's the only way
Touch the hem of his garment
Reach out to him young and old
Let him into your life
And be made whole

Home Front

The trumpet sounds and the battle cry is made
Men and women marching off to fight
Sacrificing their lives bravely and victoriously
Cry not for me, but pray for me
That the God above will keep and sustain us
We remember our homes and families
As we sit and wait, when there is quiet and
Stillness we grab a chance to meditate
For a moment we are consumed with
Peace and serenity our thoughts dancing
With memories and image of joy and
Love that awaits back at the Home front

Compassion

Compassion is Long suffering
Compassion is Endurement
Compassion is Warm
Compassion is Love
Compassion comes from Heaven
Through our father above
Caring for others , yes indeed
Compassion is what we all need

A quiet whisper

A quiet whisper
A gentle thought
A moment alone
A precious song
The quiet stillness
The awakening morn
The peace within
The love from above
A small still voice
That we often hear
The perfect solitude
That our Lord and Savior
Quietly whisper in our ear
So meek and temperate
A silent hiss from the wind
Calm words of wisdom
Is spoken to us
In a quiet whisper

Comfort

Sometimes life is hard
And our problems grow and grow
Trouble on every side
The weight of our burdens
Who can you turn to
Where can rest abide
Cast thy burdens upon
The Lord, and he shall
Sustain thee.
Psalms 55:22

The Looking Glass

To many it's a handy little gadget
It reveals truth, sometimes deception
It portrays gladness, sometimes sadness
Glass can show ugliness, or beauty
The looking glass quite beholding
But the mystery of the heart never unfolding
Jesus eyes beholds and unfolds all things
He can see into the heart
He can see into the mind
This is where our problems start
He can see into the future, as well as the pass
You see Jesus can reveal all things
Unlike the looking glass

Friendship!

Friendship is Kind
Friendship in Gentle
Friendship can hurt
Friendship can be sentimental
Friendship can be warm or it can be cold
I'm glad I've come to know you
Because you have a heart of pure gold
You're a very special person
You know the way you care
The concern you show not for yourself but for others
Your heart reflects on the outside
The Love and Compassion that dwell on the inside
Yes, Friendship is kind
Friendship is Gentle
Friends like you
We, always remember!

I'm here for you

Never feel that you are alone
When things seem to go wrong
And when you may feel that all hope has gone
Know that I'm here for you
The care and love of our friendship
Will shine bright and strong
So never feel that you are alone
You can always depend on me
That's how true friendship
Should always be

Secrets

Is it real, is it serious or make believe
precious feelings that we have shared
the special times that we spent together
and certain little things that we discuss
thoughts from our pass moments
its fun to know that the secrets
is only between the two of us

A Mother's Love

God has truly blessed us
With a rare treasure
Your love, and concern
Is far beyond measure
A precious jewel are you
Your kindness and devotion
Is shown in all that you do
We thank God and we pray
That he will richly bless you
On your special day

Fathers are special

Because God made fathers
He made them strong and dependable
With compassion and wisdom
He made them with love and care
This is why Fathers are so special
In our home, guidance and encouragement dwells
Fathers always find a way
Because father you make things well

Faith

Sorrow looks back
Worry looks around
Faith looks up
Fixing our eyes on Jesus
The Author and Finisher of our faith
Who for the joy set before him
Endured the cross despising the shame
And sat down at the right hand of the throne of God.
Hebrews 12:2

Love Connection

He died upon the cross
So my soul would not be lost
He bore my sins and shed his blood
This was an act of love
He shed tears in the garden
Hoping that he may be pardoned
But he said, not my will but thy will be done
For I am sent to do my Father's will
You see, I am his anointed son
My journey was long and hard
Only to fulfill the law of the Lord
They did not take my life but I lay it down
So that, you one day may receive your crown

Sacrifices

Sometimes there's choices we have to make
The road is paved with struggles and despair
You try to hide the pain from the ones you love
All you can do is weep silently
Wondering is there a God above
Life for you has taken a turning point
Time has been lost
You've given yourself as a sacrifice
To serve your country, whatever the cost
We proudly hold you up before our Lord
And whisper a soft prayer in his ear
Father remember our soldiers
Those far and near
Sacrifices are bitter sweet
We will keep you close to our hearts
Thanking God for your bravery
Through prayer and meditation
Until the next time we meet

Printed in the United States
by Baker & Taylor Publisher Services